So you want to marry me?

BEFORE WE SAY "I DO", WE NEED TO TALK!

EDWIN C. BASS

WESTBOW
PRESS®
A DIVISION OF THOMAS NELSON
& ZONDERVAN

WestBow Press books may be ordered through booksellers or by contacting:

WestBow Press
A Division of Thomas Nelson & Zondervan
1663 Liberty Drive
Bloomington, IN 47403
www.westbowpress.com
844-714-3454

ISBN: 979-8-3850-0202-3 (sc)
ISBN: 979-8-3850-0203-0 (hc)
ISBN: 979-8-3850-0204-7 (e)

Library of Congress Control Number: 2023912350

Print information available on the last page.

WestBow Press rev. date: 8/25/2023

DEDICATION

This book is dedicated to my wife of 52 years, Jessie Miller Bass. Like the Psalms, Jessie has been a faithful and constant source of encouragement as we traveled life together. And, dedicated to my children, Sean, Craig and Courtney along with my grandchildren, Kyng, Paige and Hannah. The privilege of being husband, father and grandfather is the greatest honor of my life. Finally, to my beloved parents, the late Bishop Joseph E. Bass, Sr. and Missionary Mary V. Bass, I offer up my gratitude for being a model for holy matrimony throughout their nearly 50 years together.

FOREWORD

Rabbi Barry R. Baron, University
Chaplain, Colgate University

Of the many transitions which people are tasked to navigate in the course of a lifetime, marriage is surely one of the trickiest, as two prospective partners, each with their own background, needs, and desires, enter into a union, intended to last a lifetime. The couple that emerges will now face life together, in a joint entity intended to provide the mutual love and support that should magnify joys and triumphs while cushioning the blows of challenges and tragedies.

Clergy in all traditions are privileged to bring partners into this sacred union while having to help people pick up the pieces of their lives in cases where that union dissolves. When a marriage fails, it often does so because the couple entered into it with insufficient knowledge of themselves and each other while lacking awareness of the mutual sacrifice and work that a marriage actually entails.

In *So You Want to Marry Me? Before we say "I do," we need to talk!* Bishop Edwin C. Bass has written a concise handbook for prospective marriage partners which can also serve as a valuable tool in the hands of clergy who counsel them and solemnize their unions. In six concise chapters (The Wedding Was Beautiful; The "Must Have" Conversations; Case Studies in Pre-Marriage Counseling; Pre-Marriage Counseling; What If We Decide to Cancel or Postpone Plans?; Coming Together with Faith), Bishop Bass employs his incisive mind, warm heart, and years of pastoral experience to lay out for readers the case for serious introspection and conversation before marriage, enabling partners to make wise choices for their lives and maximize possibilities for success in their envisioned life together. The book's five appendices form a useful and useable workbook for couples to use as an adjunct to or directly in pre-marital counseling sessions.

While he writes from the perspective of his own deep Christian faith, Bishop Bass does so in a way that makes his work readily adaptable by clergy of other faiths. In writing in this way, he demonstrates ways in which those of us interested in serious interfaith dialogue and cooperation might draw on the insights and spiritual energy of those with whom we are in continual conversation while producing a book that all might find useful.

PREFACE

How many times have you said to yourself, "If only I could have a *do over* with what I know now." In the process of living, you have learned many valuable lessons that, had you known earlier, would have had an impact on your decision making.

An important area of life that concerns many people is marriage. Failed marriages are very painful because often in retrospect the parties come to realize what could have been if only they had been more thoughtful in choosing. For those who have experienced the anguish of a failed marriage or those who wish to enter into a fulfilling marriage, learning from your own experience or that of others can help you in choosing a spouse.

This book is written for those providing pre-marriage counseling and those seeking pre-marriage counseling. It presents important questions that should be carefully considered before getting married. The questions are derived from my observations as a pastor counseling many couples both before and after marriage. Many times those in counseling are not themselves clear on the answers to these questions, let alone the answers of their potential spouse. Candid answers to the questions will give you critical insight about yourself and information about your loved one, which, if taken into consideration prior to the marriage, will lead to better decision making and ultimately fewer divorces.

It is important to learn from our personal history. So many who divorce find themselves in the same situation over and over again. If you are divorced, my best advice to you regarding your past mistakes is to thoughtfully mine the treasures of that bad experience.

Whether you have been married before or you are currently engaged or you are now married and experiencing challenges, this book will provide a means of going forward, revealing critical information that impacts compatibility and leads to either a successful or failed marriage. Alternatively, if you are simply considering the possibility of marriage in the future, this book will help you define what to look for in a potential spouse over and above physical attraction.

Furthermore, understand that failed marriages can result in failed faith. As the pastor of The Empowered Church in St. Louis, it is my firm belief that the church must equip individuals to develop fulfilling marriages leading to enhanced faith in God.

To that end, this book also delves into the marriage covenant and sheds light on what the Bible - my preference is to use the King James version - says about the sacred marriage relationship. This will be helpful to pastors as well as couples who desire to build a lasting marriage in the Christian tradition. In addition, I believe the process laid out in this book will be helpful to participants in other faith communities as well as non-believers in coming to know each other more fully.

Can two walk together, except they be agreed? – Amos 3:3

*Wisdom is the principle thing; therefore, get wisdom and
in all thy getting, get understanding. – Proverbs 4:7*

For those seeking true partnership, I hope this book will help you make a conscious, courageous, decision to develop a better understanding of each other and what goes into a fulfilling marriage, so that you are able to move forward on a stronger foundation, living each day joyfully.

CONTENTS

CHAPTER 1
The Wedding Was Beautiful!

Finally, the dream of a lifetime, you are getting married. You believe you have found the one! The future offers only the blissful fulfillment of your dreams even though, honestly, you have given little thought to whether or not those aspirations line up with the aspirations of your fiancé. In fact, you have made the frequently flawed assumption that you both want the same things.

During the courting process, each of you put forth your best foot. Fastidious attention was given to appearance and agreement on superficial matters. The response to most requests was an unhesitant "yes."

Clothes were carefully considered. Hair was perfectly coifed, make-up applied, perfume or aftershave carefully selected before each meeting. Parents and family members handled with kid gloves. Serious matters carefully avoided or, even worse, not thought relevant to the decision to get married. Absolutely nothing was allowed to get in the way of the wedding.

In most cases, more time and effort was spent on planning the actual wedding, lasting on average about thirty minutes, than on preparation for the marriage itself - thought to last for a lifetime.

Everything was intentionally positioned to appear to be perfect, a fairy tale culminating in the marriage ceremony. After everyone was in place, the bride marched in to lovely music and adoring family and friends. The groom waited, so proud of his "catch," at the altar.

The marriage ceremony started out with these words:

> "Dearly Beloved, we are gathered together here in the sight of God, and this company, to join together this man and this woman in Holy matrimony. Marriage is an honorable estate, instituted by God, blessed by our Lord Jesus Christ, and declared by Saint Paul to be honorable among men. It is not, therefore, to be entered into without Holy advice, or lightly, but reverently, soberly, advisedly, and in the fear of God. Into this holy estate, these two persons come now to be joined…"

It went on to say important words that are routinely ignored:

> "I require and charge you both, as you will answer at the dreadful day of judgment, when the secrets of all hearts shall be disclosed, that if either of you know any impediment why you may not be lawfully joined together in matrimony, you do now confess it. For be you well assured that if any persons are joined together otherwise than as God's word doth allow, their marriage is not lawful."

As so carefully planned, the marriage ceremony was beautiful and joyful and concluded with "the kiss." To the newlyweds and the audience, it appeared the future held nothing but joy and pleasure.

Encountering Reality

Tragically, my experience has shown that for many, the joy of that brief idyllic moment where time appeared to stand still was the high point of the marriage. More often than not, reality sets in within a matter of days, and couples find themselves deep in the throes and complexities of daily living.

The couples are abruptly jolted from the innocent sterile environment of superficial courting where they may know only each other's strengths, each other's most attractive features. In the intense intimacy of marriage, they see each other's weaknesses...the less-than-perfect attributes. And, they are shocked by this unanticipated, emerging information.

The gloves come off and hurtful words are exchanged without giving much concern or thought to the impact. Both parties to the marriage find themselves asking, "Who is this person?"

Valuing Candid Communication

After years of performing marriages, followed up by intense and emotional counseling sessions, I have arrived at the conclusion that most problems in marriages occur as a direct result of a failure to communicate, to fully discuss critical matters prior to the marriage and agree upon a mutually satisfactory path forward.

It is clear the best time to fully communicate and seek compromise is prior to the marriage. Afterwards, there is a sense in the offended spouse that he or she has been intentionally misled, <u>and</u> resolution becomes very difficult, if possible at all.

It is out of what I have learned through observation that I have developed a Pre-Marriage Discussion Guide designed to ensure that critical matters are fully discussed and a path forward, if possible, has been agreed upon by both parties <u>prior to marriage</u>. These are "must have" discussions for the marriage to be loving, trusting and enduring.

There is an important point I want to make here. I do not want to minimize the difficulty of having these critical discussions before marriage nor do I want to minimize the discipline required to do so. These conversations will be hard and sometimes very uncomfortable. But, my experience has made it abundantly clear that those discussions are much, much more difficult, if not impossible, after the marriage because couples feel defrauded and they simply shut down.

Although difficult, I believe there must be a complete, candid and disciplined dialogue before marriage that encompasses the complex issues that have resulted in the dissolution of so many marriages. That dialogue must be approached with the understanding that, if done well, it can have an enduring positive impact on the marriage. Alternatively, done poorly, dialogue can result in lingering unhappiness, dissatisfaction and even divorce.

Tragically, because of poor communication, too many marriages do end up in divorce, which has a powerfully negative impact on the couple divorcing. Multi-generational trauma can ensue when children are involved. Perhaps even more tragic and devastating to everyone involved are those situations where couples stay together in desolate, unfulfilled marriages where there is never true intimacy.

I came across this quote in Male Tears by Benjamin Myers[1]:

> *"The collapse of what once was had been comprised of dozens of gestures, scores of things left unsaid and hundreds of resentments spread over the thousand days that all stacked up to create millions of tiny moments of muffled misery."*

Contrary to popular thinking, all those who divorce do not hate each other. They simply cannot live together because they lack the intimacy that can only come from candid communication. Friedrich

---

[1] Male Tears, author Benjamin Myers, published April 29, 2021 by Bloomsbury Circus.

Nietzsche was on point when he said, *"It is not a lack of love, but a lack of friendship that makes unhappy marriages."*[2]

There can be no true friendship without honesty and acceptance and both are derived through candid communication. The decision to marry must go beyond "I love you" to "I know you."

Here's my best advice: slow down, ask questions and listen carefully to the answers.

---

[2] Friedrich Nietzsche, German philosopher, October 15, 1844–August 25, 1900, BrainyQuote.com, Brainy Media, Inc., 2023.

CHAPTER 2

The "Must Have" Conversations

This chapter contains the questions begging answers that are critical to establishing a successful and enduring marriage, organized into a discussion guide. *(See also a worksheet in Appendix II, which may be filled out by each prospective partner.)* There are no right or wrong answers, just honest or dishonest. Your initial reaction may be that this questionnaire is too long and will require more time than you are initially willing to give. I believe it is important for you to understand and accept this premise:

> *The magnitude of your investment of time in getting to know each other directly correlates to the likelihood of marital success. Little time spent before marriage results in little likelihood of a successful marriage.*

It may be helpful to remember that your loved one <u>will</u> ultimately learn the information you are asked to provide in the discussion guide. The only question is will it be before or after the marriage. If time is not spent before marriage, it will certainly be spent after marriage under less than favorable circumstances that are mostly argumentative and measurable in decibels.

Conducting the Conversation

The foundation of the conversation must be agreement on the following:

- You can love someone and not be compatible with that person.
- The more you know about your potential spouse the higher the likelihood of marital success.
- When disagreements are revealed, it is possible to define the problem and, with counseling, to work toward a solution that is acceptable to both of you.
- Those who decide not to proceed at the conclusion of counseling, because they could not resolve their differences, avoid a potentially damaging situation that in all likelihood would have ended up in divorce or an acrimonious marriage.
- Regardless of the outcome, both individuals will emerge better off even though it may not feel that way immediately.

The Bible gives some guidance into how the conversation must be conducted. In the Apostle Paul's letter to the Ephesian church found in the book of Ephesians, chapter 4, verse 15, he uses words that I believe beautifully express how this critical conversation must unfold.

> *But speaking the truth in love,....*
> – King James Bible

> *Rather, let our lives lovingly express truth [in all things, speaking truly, living truly].*
> – The Amplified Bible

I encourage you to follow these guidelines:

- Invite God's presence into the conversation by starting with prayer.

- As you engage in this critical conversation, remember to be kind to each other even at emotional moments of intense disagreement. Seek to choose words carefully. Do not respond with emotional outburst when some new information is disclosed.
- Take time apart to become calm and think about it. Think of possible solutions.
- Continue the process through to the end no matter what you hear. Give each other a chance to lay out their concerns. Try to identify or define the problem.
- Get back together to work toward a solution that is acceptable to both of you. Ask for mediation if you need help.
- Remember that this is someone you love.
- Express gratitude for answers you received, realizing how difficult in many cases it was to give them.
- Close out each session with prayer.

The Pre-Marriage Discussion Guide

These are the questions that are critical to establishing an enduring marriage. Once the worksheet *(see Appendix II)* is completed, the answers to these questions will only be seen by the husband and wife candidates unless the decision is made jointly to seek assistance in resolving conflicts.

The Marriage

- What is your current marital status?
- If divorced, what was the contributing issue(s)? How can you ensure it will not impact your impending marriage?
- In your own words, what does marriage mean to you?
- What specific actions or behaviors would fulfill marriage as you perceive it should be?

- What are your expectations for the marriage? First year? Long term?
- With regard to commitment to this marriage, what things would cause the marriage to dissolve emotionally or legally?

Money and Property

- Where will we live after the marriage?
- How will you handle your money? Individual bank accounts? Joint bank accounts?
- How will household expenses be shared?
- What kind of expenditures should be approved by both parties in advance?
- Do you believe in saving? How will you ensure saving goals will be met?
- How will you handle property attained prior to marriage, e.g. real estate, cash, cars, investments, etc.?
- How will you handle requests for loans from your family members? From friends?

Work

- Does your future spouse have a job? Will he/she continue to work after you are married? What is your expectation regarding his or her work, e.g. hours worked?
- What has been your track record relative to holding a job?
- Do you plan to work during the marriage and what is your expectation, e.g. hours worked?

Education

- What is the highest level of education you have attained?
- Do you plan to continue your pursuit of education?

- How do you intend to pay for it?
- Will you be a part-time or full-time student?
- If full-time, will not working be acceptable to your spouse?

Spending

- How would you quantify your expenditures directly related to the courtship? Please consider the applicable categories for those expenditures: Meals in restaurants, entertainment (e.g. movies, concerts), travel, and other.
- Are you expecting those expenditures to continue after the marriage ceremony? At the same or different level?
- Is shopping an important aspect of your life?
- Percentage wise how would you quantify your spending by category? For now, consider the categories of clothing, food, travel, gifts and charitable giving.
- In the marriage, do you expect your expenditures in those categories will continue at the same levels? Be reduced substantially?

Physical Relationship

- Do you agree that it is a fact that your appearance and that of your spouse will change as you age? How will you deal with the physical changes?
- Will you still love him or her? Are you concerned that your spouse's feelings may change if your appearance changes? Do you feel strongly that your love can endure through all the inevitable changes?
- In terms of personal hygiene what are your expectations for your spouse?
- As clearly as possible, in words you are comfortable with, what are your expectations of the sexual aspects of marriage? This is not the time to be shy or reticent.

- What sexual acts are you uncomfortable with performing?
- With regard to your sexual relationship, how will you deal with differences in expectations and levels of comfort?
- Do you watch pornography/graphic sex?
- How will you feel if your spouse watches pornography?
- Have you been subjected to sexual, physical and/or emotional abuse at any time? Have you received care to address this trauma?
- Do you define yourself as heterosexual? Bi-Sexual? Homosexual?
- Are there any issues relative to sexual identity that you need to disclose? Has there been a time when you experienced internal struggle over your sexual preference or gender identification?
- Do you have any questions about your future spouse's sexual identity?

Communications

- Are you satisfied with the level of communication/conversation between the two of you now?
- With regard to communication/conversation, how would you describe it?
- What do you talk about when you are together?
- What topics important to you are not talked about?
- Do you feel you do most of the listening?
- Do you have shared interests, hobbies or activities? Please list.
- How will you handle inevitable conflicts with each other? With family members? With others?
- What is your plan for ensuring you keep open dialogue throughout the marriage?

The Family

- List all your children including adults and grandchildren.
- Do either of you have dependent children that will live with you and your spouse? Do you have a visitation plan that involves the dependent child's parent?
- Do you plan to have children together? How many? When?
- Do you have any physical issues that would preclude having children? If yes, what are they?
- If you find you're unable to conceive as a couple, how will this affect your relationship? Will you consider adoption?
- What are your beliefs about disciplining children?
- When needed, how will discipline be accomplished?
- Will others be allowed to discipline your children, e.g., family members, friends, etc.?
- If applicable, how do you feel about your husband/wife disciplining your children by another man/woman? Has your agreement been communicated to those children?

Your Extended Family

- Who are your parents? Are they still living?
- How would you describe your relationship with your father?
- How would you describe your relationship with your mother?
- Do you have siblings? If so, describe your relationship with each sibling.
- How would you describe your relationship with your grandparents?
- Share a significant memory of each of your parents, grandparents and siblings.
- How will you deal with your spouse's parents? With his/her children and grandchildren? With his/her siblings?

- What is your expectation regarding where you will spend holidays?
- How will the two of you establish your own family's customs?

Religion

- What is your religious affiliation? What is your spiritual status?
- How often do you attend church? How much time weekly do you spend in church/religious activities? Will this change after the marriage?
- How do you feel about your spouse's time commitment to participating in church/religious activities?
- Have you committed your life to Christ? Why or why not?
- If your spouse does not share your religious beliefs or has not made a commitment to Christ, how will you deal with the inevitable conflict?
- Have you studied Biblical teachings regarding marriage? (*See Chapter 6: Coming Together with Faith.*) Which of these Bible verses are important to you? Are there verses that you are concerned about applying in your marriage?
- Are there activities that you are expected to participate in with your future spouse that conflict with your spiritual beliefs? Does he or she understand and accept your position?

Financial Disclosure

- How much debt do you currently have? Delineate amounts and sources. Include any personal loans, mortgages, credit cards, unsecured loans, alimony, child support and any informal/formal agreements you have entered into to provide financial support.
- Do you currently have any liens or unsettled judgments? Explain.

- Attach a copy of your credit report (current within the last 30 days).
- My credit rating is: excellent, good, fair, or poor. Is there anything omitted from the credit report that should be disclosed?
- Have you ever filed for bankruptcy? When? Status?
- Are you current on state and federal income tax returns and payments? If not, explain.
- Are you under tax audit or a payment plan with either state or federal?
- Disclose any bad financial behaviors that you have practiced in the past and your current thinking and practices pertaining to those past practices.
- Do you have life insurance? Who are the beneficiaries? Will this change after marriage?
- How will assets accumulated before the marriage be distributed upon your death? Do you have a will?
- How will assets accumulated during our marriage be distributed?

Political Affiliation

- How do you classify your political affiliation?
- Do you have any strongly held political opinions?
- If your opinions differ from those of your future spouse, how will you manage the inevitable conflicts?

Housework and Property Maintenance

- What is your expectation regarding who will take care of day-to-day routine housework and maintenance (cooking, cleaning, washing dishes, mowing, etc.)?
- How much time do you anticipate you will spend on these tasks each week?

Medical/Health

- Do you have any on-going medical (physical and/or mental health) conditions?
- Do you need to take prescribed medications?
- Do you have any conditions that may preclude you from having children or performing sexually?
- Are you now, or have you been, in recovery for an addiction? If so, explain any support that would be helpful to you.

Criminal History

- Have you ever been arrested? If yes, why? When?
- Have you served time in prison? If yes, why? When?
- Do you currently have any outstanding issues of a criminal nature?
- Attach a copy of your police report current within the last 30 days.

Reflections

- If you could change anything about your past what would it be?
- Do you have aspirations that you still hope to achieve?
- Is there anything you can think of that might become a source of dispute in the future? Please disclose.
- In what way do you hope to enhance your future spouse's life? How has he/she enhanced your life so far?

See Appendix II for a worksheet to copy for each person to fill out and share with each other. That information will only be seen by the couple unless they decide to seek assistance in resolving conflicts.

As a marriage counselor, if requested, I will serve as a mediator. Note that in this role, I will facilitate the exchange of all documents shared, including divorce decrees, death certificates, medical records and police reports, but I will not view them.

CHAPTER 3

Case Studies in Pre-Marriage Counseling

These case studies illustrate the value of investing in communications.

Case Study #1

For the purpose of maintaining anonymity in this case study, we identify our case study subjects with the pseudonyms, "George and Martha." George is a 48 year old man and has never been married before. Martha is 50 years old and she has been married before with adult children by her former husband.

After going through the rigorous pre-marriage process, George and Martha arrived at the church on the scheduled date of their marriage ceremony and informed me that in the process they discovered their differences were too great to reconcile and they decided amicably to not proceed with the wedding. I considered this to be a successful conclusion to the process, forestalling conflict and divorce down the road.

Case Study #2

For the purpose of maintaining anonymity in this case study, we identify our case study subject with the pseudonym, "Cedric." He is currently in his retirement years. Cedric was previously divorced but now enjoys an enduring and successful marriage and sound relationships with their adult children.

Based on his experience, Cedric possesses significant insight into the underlying root causes and factors in matrimonial success or failure. He is remarkably transparent and highly motivated to share both his plus and minus life experiences in order to enlighten others and minimize detrimental life choices.

1. *With regard to your first marriage, do you believe you were prepared to marry?*

   Absolutely not.

2. *Why not?*

   For one thing, I was much too young and immature to make that major life decision. My parents had a great marriage that lasted for many decades, but they didn't talk much about it to us kids. Knowing little about the nuts and bolts of marital success, I naturally assumed that marriage would be easy and work similarly for me. I grew up in a tremendous church that emphasized Godliness and permanence in marriage. But they didn't offer much in the way of relationship instruction, and no pre-marital counseling was available.

3. *In retrospect, did you really know your wife when you married her?*

   I married my childhood sweetheart in my early twenties. We grew up in the same neighborhood and attended the same church. Anyone observing us would have naturally assumed that we were familiar with every aspect of each other's life. But no, we didn't really know each other as we should have. Far too many young marriages fail because both parties are clueless about what to expect. During my youth, the media portrayed marriage as a carefree and romantic fantasy. Loving husbands diligently worked nine-to-five and came home to beautiful wives wearing pearl necklaces and dressed as if they were on their way to some church service, with delicious dinner awaiting in the oven. Those television caricatures of marriage were completely fictional and did not match the reality of life in African-American communities. My wife and I knew more about the "images" that the media and the church culture had painted, more so than we knew about ourselves. Unfortunately, we didn't invest the time, energy and planning that is essential for success.

4. *What things about her were you surprised to learn after getting married?*

Early on, we had an amazing degree of physical attraction and passion, which drew us close together. I had no idea that this could or would change over time. It did. Not knowing that love is a decision, I was sure that my wife and I loved each other far less or not at all when those fires of intimacy began to smolder. I clearly remember the night before our wedding when my oldest sister tried her best to counsel me. She said that sexual intimacy is a dangerous trap for the young and it produces a kind of hypnosis that causes people to feel sure that they are in *love*, when likely they are more in *lust*. I felt sick to my stomach all that night, but my pride, my desire to honor my commitment, and the dreaded thought of hurting my wife-to-be caused me to proceed with wedding plans.

5. *In retrospect, can you say you really knew yourself when you got married?*

No, not at all. I was sort of a smart dude with the books. But I was profoundly ignorant about life. I assumed that the world was my oyster and it was impossible for me to fail. That mindset didn't serve me well, and there was little motivation to look more deeply into myself. In my view, I was a Christian. My wife was a Christian. And we would definitely have a great education, with a beautiful home, cars, kids, church and a happy family life.

6. *What things about yourself were you surprised to learn after getting married?*

To be honest, I was extremely surprised that I found myself attracted to women other than my wife. Our early relationship had been so passionate that it never dawned on me that I would "see" anyone else. For the most part, those relationships were fantasy, not reality. But I have to confess that on one occasion I failed and strayed from my vow of fidelity. It's something that has continually haunted my conscience and impacted my self-worth.

7. *What have you learned from your past marriage?*

It took me quite a while to discover that effective communication is the cornerstone of any and all relationships. Clear, open, honest dialogue is mission critical. I really wish someone wise had mentored us, and we had been receptive to it. I wish someone had taught us how to talk to one another and to listen to one another, especially during those inevitable bumps in the road. In time, I learned that marriage is actually a partnership. My early tendency was to be somewhat domineering. Now I'm keenly aware that God created us to have dominion in the earth, not over each other.

8. *What were the contributors to the failure of the marriage?*

Being too young and immature was the first cause. Mutual infidelity was another. Discussing internal problems with outsiders and listening to wrong voices and fleshly solutions was another. Not developing financial consensus, consistency and strategies was another.

9. *What was the aftermath of your divorce?*

How can I describe what divorce does? It even feels like death. The five stages of grief are there. It's way bigger than the signing of a legal document. It is the death and burial of a dream. It's the nagging feeling that all is lost. And it's not only a near death experience for the spouses, it is destructive beyond measure for the whole family. A psychologist friend told me about its collateral damage − that half of children of divorces enter adulthood worried, scared, confused and angry. I've seen it first-hand. It haunts and hurts so many people, for years to come.

10. *What would you do differently if you had a do over?*

I would definitely marry at a much older age. Most men are too immature and incomplete to marry before their mid-thirties. That might seem to be an extreme delay to some, but we men should have time to understand ourselves, to complete our education and to develop a career before taking on the covenant of caring for a wife and children. I have similar views about women, although it does seem that they mature and settle down much earlier. Importantly, prior to marriage, I would proactively purge myself from any "ghost images" of failed relationships (mine or others) via intensive counseling.

11. *What were the things that drew you into the marriage?*

Sexuality and sex were major drawing cards. Growing up in the church, I had extremely powerful convictions that pre-marital sex was anathema. I still believe it is because of the resultant soul ties. The inevitable heavy petting of young people can be a gateway to pre-marital sex. For young Christians, the resultant guilt, shame and overarching desire to live right could lead to a decision to wed long before there is sufficient emotional maturity.

12. *How does that compare with what became important to you after marriage?*

The most important things after our marriage had begun, especially years later, were maintaining an atmosphere of mutual trust, communicating clearly and respectfully, and developing a close and fulfilling friendship.

13. *Were your finances a concern during the past marriage?*

This is somewhat of a sore spot for me. There were times when we seemed to be living on top of the world. But there were other times when our finances were slim or scarce. Inconsistency was the issue. It is my firm belief that a huge percentage of arguments and break-ups occur due to money matters.

14. *What have you done and what are you doing in your current marriage that is making a difference?*

I'm a much better listener now and I feel certain that I have developed more respect and empathy for women in general. My current wife and I are on the same page spiritually, that is, we often enter into fervent prayer, worship and study of the Word together. We make shared decisions about all family and financial matters. The net difference is that I've gotten older and wiser.

15. *Out of your marital experience, what advice do you give to your children?*

a. Take time to get to know yourself before you join in life with someone else.

b. Complete your education and get a leg up in your career prior to marriage.

c. Don't even think about getting married without very extensive counseling.

d. Put Christ first; that is, in all your ways, acknowledge and consult with Him.

e. No other human being is ever more important than your spouse.

f. Make your spouse your closest and dearest friend.

g. Budget, spend, invest and save – wisely and consistently.

h. Develop marriage and family goals, with annual evaluations and revisions.

i. The family is the basic building block of the Kingdom of God.

Case Study #3

For the purpose of maintaining anonymity, we identify our case study subjects with the pseudonyms, "Anthony and Theresa." Anthony is a 27-year-old man who has never been married before. Theresa is also 27 years of age. She has never been married but she does have a son, Damon, by a prior relationship. The father is active in her son's life. Damon will live with Anthony and Theresa after they are married.

Session with Anthony and Theresa

In the course of pre-marriage counseling, they found that they had generally agreed upon most of the critical issues in the course of dating. They did, however, encounter disagreement on the issue of how Anthony would interact with Theresa's son once they married.

Theresa felt strongly that raising her son should continue to be the exclusive responsibility of her and the boy's father. She informed Anthony that he should not direct or correct Damon. She emphasized that she and the boy's father were pleased with the results they had achieved so far. They remained committed to constant communication to ensure that they would continue to be successful in that regard.

Anthony had a problem with the plan on two counts. First, while he realized that there would be communication between Theresa and Damon's father, he felt it was too often and sometimes too personal. He had overheard their conversations on more than one occasion and found them to go far beyond a discussion of Damon and his well-being, venturing into personal and intimate matters that he felt should only be shared with him. Second, he felt that if Damon lived with him, he should have some say in raising him and that both Damon and his father should be told as much.

Suddenly the calm waters became turbulent. From Theresa's point of view, all was going so well until this can of worms was opened. Her anger at both Anthony and me was palpable.

At this point, I separated them for individual sessions.

Session with Anthony

Meeting with Anthony, I gave him a chance to lay out his concerns. This is what he said: "I love Damon and want the best for him. I don't see how he can have a respectful relationship with me if he sees me as an adult he lives with having no value to impart in his life and no authority to provide correction as needed. Makes me look like I'm just in this for a booty call."

He went on to say, "With regard to Theresa's relationship with Damon's father, I would be comfortable with it if conversations were limited to Damon. And, if Theresa kept me fully informed where and when those conversations occurred."

I acknowledged his feelings as being valid. I explained that he must acknowledge the success that Theresa and Damon's father had achieved with Damon. He was a good kid, doing well in school and respectful of his peers and others. In doing so, Anthony might achieve a level of calm in which Theresa would listen to his concerns. He promised to think about it.

Session with Theresa

Before proceeding I had to deal with Theresa's anger with me and with Anthony. I asked her point blank, "Are you upset with me?"

Trying hard to remain respectful, she said, "We were doing fine until you talked us into marital counseling so yeah, I am upset with you."

I responded by saying, "Theresa, you and Anthony came to my office and indicated you wanted to get married and asked me to preside over the wedding. I told you I would be honored to do so but I have one stipulation – the two of you would have to complete marital counseling. You agreed, correct?"

Theresa, "Yes but...."

Interrupting, I said, "I was very clear in detailing why I believe in and insist upon marital counseling before I will perform a marriage. Right?"

Theresa acknowledged that was true.

"Theresa, while disagreement is not pleasant, you should be appreciative of the fact that this disagreement, which would certainly have emerged after the wedding, is being discussed now. You have an opportunity to work toward a solution that is acceptable to both of you. To do so, you have to acknowledge that he has legitimate concerns and open your mind to finding a way forward. My way or the highway is not a way forward. Will you calmly listen to what he has to say?"

Final Counseling Session with Anthony and Theresa

I reminded them that the reason they were in my office was because they indicated they loved each other and wanted to spend their lives together in marriage. I tasked them with the assignment to find a time and a place where they could calmly and completely hear each other out. I cautioned them on the importance of choosing words in the conversation carefully and the danger of inflexibility.

The Outcome

Returning to my office a week later, Anthony and Theresa informed me that they remembered how much they loved each other. They also indicated that neither of them could envision a life without the other. From that starting point, they sought a way forward.

Here's what they decided:

1. Anthony would never take the place of Damon's father, but Anthony would be encouraged to develop an active role in Damon's upbringing that would allow him to be a 2nd dad and pour into him love, direction and correction. Both Anthony and Theresa agreed that this would work only if the two of them had constant candid conversation, remaining open to adjustments as warranted.

2. With regard to Damon's father, Theresa agreed that she would limit communication to rearing Damon and that she would keep Anthony fully appraised of all interactions. If an in-person meeting was needed between Theresa and Damon's father, Anthony would be informed in advance and given the option of attending if he wished.

Anthony and Theresa had a beautiful wedding over which I presided. From all appearances, they are enjoying a loving and fulfilling marriage.

CHAPTER 4
Pre-Marriage Counseling

This chapter explains the process that I use in marriage counseling before conducting a wedding so that candidates will know what to expect from the start. Pastors will find this chapter helpful in carrying out one of their most critical and sacred responsibilities.

In the Christian tradition, marriage is styled after the church in this respect. The husband is instructed to give himself to the marriage as Christ gave Himself to the church. The Bible informs us that "the gates of hell shall not prevail against the church." Knowing this, Satan continues to execute a strategy that can impact the church indirectly and that is to literally war against God-sanctioned marriage.

Unhappy people tend to lose faith. Likewise, failed marriages can lead many to question their faith and, in some cases, abandon their faith. And, many others (not just the husband and wife) can be adversely impacted collaterally by failed marriages.

I believe the church must respond with thorough pre-marriage counseling that will equip individuals to address issues and make sound decisions prior to marriage, which will lead to fulfilling marriages and enhanced faith in God. In fact, I will not perform the marriage ceremony unless this process is satisfactorily completed because my experience indicates those that do not complete the process have a high rate of post-ceremony problems including but not limited to divorce.

I have found that utilizing the counseling approach laid out in this book results in a measurable reduction in the rate of divorce. I encourage individuals who provide pre-marital counseling to informally track outcomes relative to longevity and divorce as a means of evaluating effectiveness.

Pre-Marriage Counseling Steps

1. Read and discuss Coming Together with Faith *(see Chapter 6)* to understand what the Bible says about marriage.
2. Complete the "Must Have Conversations" process.

    a. Each of you completes The Pre-Marriage Discussion Guide worksheet independently over a two-week period. *(See Appendix II.)*
    b. After completion, share your answers with each other to identify areas of agreement <u>and</u> areas of conflict/ differences to talk through. You may find it helpful to use the table provided *(see Appendix III)* to capture the details regarding any concerns/differences that you need to work through.
    c. Attempt to reconcile areas of conflict/differences in conversation over a three-week period or as long as necessary. This work of speaking candidly and actively listening can be very emotional and challenging. Please remember the importance of choosing words carefully and being flexible.
    d. Consider your option to involve the pastor in mediating conflicts/differences that you have not been able to resolve. In some cases the result is a clear agreement to disagree

so mediation is not requested. Be aware that issue is more than likely to come up over and over in the future.

3. Reach a decision to stop or proceed. It is not an easy thing to decide which way to go as you encounter the swirl of information and emotion in this process. Do we part ways here or do we go on? Can our relationship become what we both want? Can we work through the issues? As we do, will our love survive?

4. Inform the pastor of your thinking at this point and if the decision is to continue with your plan to marry, proceed with the following steps.

5. Develop a Marriage Mission Statement and draft your marriage vows (see *Appendix IV*).

   a. Each of you draft a summary of the aims and values of the marriage.
   b. Work together to merge the content into one statement, reconciling any differences.
   c. Review the traditional and sample personalized marriage vows. Draft your personalized vows, if desired.

6. Begin developing your first-year budget *(see Appendix V)*.

7. Pastor meets with husband candidate for practical discussion.

8. Pastor's wife, or female counselor, meets with wife candidate for practical discussion.

9. Meet in a final joint session with your pastor.

   a. Thoroughly review your marriage vows to ensure you both fully understand the commitment you are making.
   b. Confirm your decision to proceed with the marriage or go your separate ways.
   c. If the decision is to marry, discuss your personal wishes regarding the marriage ceremony including finalizing the marriage vows.

CHAPTER 5

What If We Decide to Cancel or Postpone Plans?

The primary purpose of pre-marriage counseling is to implement an organized, thorough and strategic plan for prospective spouses to connect with biblical and experiential wisdom and to thereby invest deep and serious thought into the choices and conditions that should come before and during a successful marriage. This rigorous counseling is designed to move the candidates toward a practical end-point that is favorable and feasible for *both parties*.

Inherent in the process are two possible outcomes:

- The possibility that candidates decide to proceed with their marriage, concluding after full disclosure that the lives of each will be enhanced and elevated in union with the other.
- The possibility that couples will find their differences irreconcilable and choose not to proceed with the marriage.

In my counseling, I have witnessed both outcomes. In my opinion either outcome is a success and the participants should be truly commended for investing time and patience in reaching this end point.

As a tenured pastor, I am keenly aware that a decision to call the marriage off can be quite challenging for both parties. Their engagement has likely been publicly proclaimed and celebrated. Family and friends typically have been notified and consulted. Wedding plans might have been made, contracts signed. And in some cases, invitations have actually been printed and mailed.

If there is a need to delay or cancel wedding plans, the potential partners are prone to feel a degree of embarrassment. So what should be done?

First of all, there is an overarching need for both parties to be completely honest and candid regarding their conclusions and feelings. While diplomacy is always in order, candor must reign in this mission-critical life decision. Bottom-line: it is far better to experience momentary discomfort than to enter into a binding covenant with the wrong partner that could be result in considerable pain, disillusionment, resentment, or even divorce. So be sure to share your "real" thoughts and feelings – respectfully, clearly and honestly.

Secondly, offer the gift of unconditional love and understanding to each other. That is, refuse to enter into narrow, negative and judgmental thinking, or to allow any harsh words to emerge from your mouth. If you were truly friends in the first place, you must maintain mutual respect, compassion and honor. Consider the words of the Apostle Paul in his letter to the Ephesians, chapter 4, verse 32:

> *And be ye kind one to another, tenderhearted, forgiving one another, even as God for Christ's sake hath forgiven you.*

You must keep your pastor and/or counselor in the loop. Let them know exactly where you are at this important moment in time so they can offer guidance.

In addition, inform your close family members and friends of any change in plans. And never allow *anyone* to exert pressure in the direction of advancing wedding plans that you are convinced should not occur at this time or not at all. Remember that forgiveness does not demand that you proceed in a marriage that you have determined is not in your best interest.

I encourage you to walk with your heads held high. Both of you have demonstrated profound wisdom, courage and character by your ability to be reasonable and objective about yourself and the possibility of a shared life with one another.

Finally, who knows what the future holds? A delay could be simply the opportunity to strengthen the foundation of your relationship. Alternatively, a decision to go your separate ways opens up the opportunity to meet the person you should marry. Forgive the past. Be prayerful about the future.

CHAPTER 6

Coming Together with Faith

Because we live in a "free" society, which is becoming increasingly more secular in outlook, many would balk at the idea that there can only be *one way* to do anything. However, as a product of the Judeo-Christian tradition, my belief is that Almighty God, the Creator of all, has both the right and the responsibility to establish the divine order for His creation.

As the Bible reveals, *"the earth is the Lord's, and the fullness thereof; the world and they that dwell therein"* (Psalm 24:1). The omniscient, self-existent, eternal God created Adam and Eve with the foreknowledge that they would be joined together through the holy marriage covenant which has three partnering pillars: God, man and woman.

Understand that in referring to "the divine order," I am aware that this concept is reflected in various religious traditions. For example, the Talmud states that *"a man should love his wife as much as he loves himself, and honour her more than he honours himself."* And I'm sure you can find similar beliefs regarding the sanctity of marriage in other holy books. But in this chapter, I offer my thoughts on illuminating Bible passages from my perspective as a Christian pastor.

I do believe that the increasing secularization of society is having a negative impact on the nuclear family. The lack of a foundation built on the immutable principles of the Bible continues to shift our society to one based on the humanistic thinking of the day. When right and wrong become subject to prevailing winds, the family loses its bridge from generation to generation resulting in a drastic breakdown in communication. When communication within families declines, unity suffers. When unity within families suffers, society at large declines. It becomes a synergistic decline where the decline in family exacerbates the decline in society <u>and</u> the decline in society accelerates the decline in the family.

While I strongly believe that commitment to the foundation of Christian faith dramatically increases the likelihood of a successful marriage, I do acknowledge that there are successful marriages (as men would evaluate success) amongst participants in other faith communities as well as non-believers. Without reservation, I believe in and adhere to the tenets of Christian faith. With that said, my go-to for direction and clarification is the Holy Bible, (specifically, the King James version) recognizing that many who seek to marry do not share that belief.

Genesis 1:27

So God created man in his own image, in the image of God created he him; male and female created he them.

> From the very beginning, the divine plan for marriage was the population of the earth and the continuation of humankind. Thus, God's marching orders to the first family were, "be fruitful... multiply...replenish the earth...subdue it...and have dominion." (Genesis 1:28)

Genesis 2:18

It is not good that the man should be alone; I will make him an help meet for him.

> Man and woman were purposefully created by God to be together. Marriage is the ultimate expression of

God's creative genius. Clearly implicit in The Holy Writ is the fundamental fact that Almighty God, as the creator of humankind, established and blessed the covenant of marriage via our fore-parents, Adam and Eve. Some skeptics question this since the Word contains no formal marriage ceremony. However, the sacrament of holy matrimony is firmly established by divine actions and directives.

Genesis 2:24

Therefore shall a man leave his father and his mother, and shall cleave unto his wife: and they shall be one flesh.

Within the covenant of marriage, a man and a woman mystically become one, which is the divine order. This spiritual union is divinely ordered and entirely unique. Indeed, there is no relationship in the human experience that is remotely comparable to or greater than marriage.

1 Corinthians 11:9-12

[9] Neither was the man created for the woman; but the woman for the man.

[10] For this cause ought the woman to have power on her head because of the angels.

[11] Nevertheless neither is the man without the woman, neither the woman without the man, in the Lord.

[12] For as the woman is of the man, even so is the man also by the woman; but all things of God.

It is mission-critical to understand and to accept the spiritual interdependency that is the foundation and fabric of marriage. This partnership is entirely distinctive because it is both God-ordered and God-defined in order to fulfill divine purpose.

Ephesians 5:21-33

21 Submitting yourselves one to another in the fear of God.

22 Wives, submit yourselves unto your own husbands, as unto the Lord.

23 For the husband is the head of the wife, even as Christ is the head of the church: and he is the savior of the body.

24 Therefore as the church is subject unto Christ, so let the wives be to their own husbands in every thing.

25 Husbands, love your wives, even as Christ also loved the church, and gave himself for it;

26 That he might sanctify and cleanse it with the washing of water by the word,

27 That he might present it to himself a glorious church, not having spot, or wrinkle, or any such thing; but that it should be holy and without blemish.

28 So ought men to love their wives as their own bodies. He that loveth his wife loveth himself.

29 For no man ever yet hated his own flesh; but nourisheth and cherisheth it, even as the Lord the church:

30 For we are members of his body, of his flesh, and of his bones.

31 For this cause shall a man leave his father and mother, and shall be joined unto his wife, and they two shall be one flesh.

32 This is a great mystery: but I speak concerning Christ and the church.

33 Nevertheless let every one of you in particular so love his wife even as himself; and the wife see that she reverence her husband.

Just as Christ dearly loved humankind and vicariously took upon Himself the penalty for sin, experiencing the traumatic substitutionary atonement, so the husband must love his wife so completely that he is ready, willing and able to offer his very life for her well-being.

It is important to note that effective and enduring order cannot exist unless it is first fully defined and then operationalized. It is God, not us, who defines and directs this sacred order. According to the Word, the husband is the head of the home and the wife is his helper. This does not grant permission for the husband to be overbearing or controlling - quite the contrary. He is to be completely submissive to Christ and to lovingly lead his wife and family, by precept and example.

1 Peter 3:7

7 Likewise, ye husbands, dwell with them according to knowledge, giving honour unto the wife, as unto the weaker vessel, and as being heirs together of the grace of life; that your prayers be not hindered.

A Godly husband understands the divinely crafted family order. He engages his wife lovingly, peacefully and prayerfully. This wise family leadership approach truly honors his wife, while maximizing supernatural blessings on their offspring and household. For in the midst of such harmony and unity of purpose, the third covenant partner to the marriage, Almighty God, endows special and sustained benediction.

1 Corinthians 7:3-4

³ Let the husband render unto the wife due benevolence: and likewise also the wife unto the husband.

⁴ The wife hath not power of her own body, but the husband: and likewise also the husband hath not power of his own body, but the wife.

> While procreation is unquestionably a key intention and component of the marriage covenant, this gift can be fulfilled through adoption. The Creator has also graciously granted the gift of emotional and physical intimacy with mutual and lasting fulfillment. Both partners should do their best to nurture and sustain this close bond, which lends itself to continual closeness, joy, stability and fidelity.

Matthew 18:19

¹⁹ Again I say unto you, That if two of you shall agree on earth as touching any thing that they shall ask, it shall be done for them of my Father which is in heaven.

> This powerful promise in Scripture speaks of the ability and potential for loving and spiritually intimate couples to accomplish anything and everything together. In fact, in His immutable Word, the infallible God promises to act in concert and in full support of their highest dreams and aspirations. According to the Word, we can do all things through

Christ (Philippians 4:13). Within the covenant of marriage, the divine intention is for the husband and wife to accomplish "all [of these] things" through an extremely positive, purposeful and productive partnership.

Psalm 127:1

¹Except the Lord build the house, they labor in vain that build it: except the Lord keep the city, the watchman waketh but in vain.

When the marriage covenant is constructed on the bedrock of obedience and submission to God, it will not only survive, it will thrive, and overcome any obstacle or challenge.

1 Peter 3:1

¹Likewise, ye wives, be in subjection to your own husbands; that, if any obey not the word, they also may without the word be won by the conversation of the wives;

While the Word maintains that we should not be "unequally yoked together with unbelievers," sometimes one marriage partner may come to Christ before the other (II Corinthians 6:14). Generally speaking, women seem to find it easier to accept and submit to our sovereign Savior. Sometimes, this example serves as a powerful and effective witness to an unbelieving husband – to the extent that he will eventually believe, receive and follow Jesus Christ. This principle may also be applicable in marriages where both partners are saved. The unique love and kindness that a wife is capable of can become the catalyst for an increasing level of spiritual maturity in her husband.

Proverbs 31:10-31

[10] Who can find a virtuous woman? for her price is far above rubies.

[11] The heart of her husband doth safely trust in her, so that he shall have no need of spoil.

[12] She will do him good and not evil all the days of her life.

[13] She seeketh wool, and flax, and worketh willingly with her hands.

[14] She is like the merchants' ships; she bringeth her food from afar.

[15] She riseth also while it is yet night, and giveth meat to her household, and a portion to her maidens.

[16] She considereth a field, and buyeth it: with the fruit of her hands she planteth a vineyard.

[17] She girdeth her loins with strength, and strengtheneth her arms.

[18] She perceiveth that her merchandise is good: her candle goeth not out by night.

[19] She layeth her hands to the spindle, and her hands hold the distaff.

[20] She stretcheth out her hand to the poor; yea, she reacheth forth her hands to the needy.

[21] She is not afraid of the snow for her household: for all her household are clothed with scarlet.

[22] She maketh herself coverings of tapestry; her clothing is silk and purple.

23 Her husband is known in the gates, when he sitteth among the elders of the land.

24 She maketh fine linen, and selleth it; and delivereth girdles unto the merchant.

25 Strength and honour are her clothing; and she shall rejoice in time to come.

26 She openeth her mouth with wisdom; and in her tongue is the law of kindness.

27 She looketh well to the ways of her household, and eateth not the bread of idleness.

28 Her children arise up, and call her blessed; her husband also, and he praiseth her.

29 Many daughters have done virtuously, but thou excellest them all.

30 Favour is deceitful, and beauty is vain: but a woman that feareth the Lord, she shall be praised.

31 Give her of the fruit of her hands; and let her own works praise her in the gates.

Absolutely nothing can remotely approach the value of a virtuous woman who wisely considers and cares for her husband and children, acting faithfully and consistently on their behalf. Her diligent works demand great respect and recognition in the home and community, all of which accrue to the benefit of her husband.

Proverbs 5:18-23

18 Let thy fountain be blessed: and rejoice with the wife of thy youth.

19 Let her be as the loving hind and pleasant roe; let her breasts satisfy thee at all times; and be thou ravished always with her love.

²⁰ And why wilt thou, my son, be ravished with a strange woman, and embrace the bosom of a stranger?

²¹ For the ways of man are before the eyes of the LORD, and he pondereth all his goings.

²² His own iniquities shall take the wicked himself, and he shall be holden with the cords of his sins.

²³ He shall die without instruction; and in the greatness of his folly he shall go astray.

> Contemporary times find some men abandoning their wives in search of ostensibly more attractive and younger mates. Such an unwise course of action fails to take seriously the priceless years of shared life experiences and lessons learned. The shared journey is incomparable and thus cannot be replaced or duplicated. When covenant partners view their marriage and each other through the wise eyes of God's love, mercy and grace, their love flowers and matures, having endured the twin tests of time and circumstances.

Matthew 19:6-9

⁶ Wherefore they are no more twain, but one flesh. What therefore God hath joined together, let not man put asunder.

⁷ They say unto him, Why did Moses then command to give a writing of divorcement, and to put her away?

⁸ He saith unto them, Moses because of the hardness of your hearts suffered you to put away your wives: but from the beginning it was not so.

⁹ And I say unto you, Whosoever shall put away his wife, except it be for fornication, and shall marry another, committeth adultery: and whoso marrieth her which is put away doth commit adultery.

> In marriage, two have become one. This spiritual relationship blessed by God is permanent and can only be severed by adultery.

Mark 10:11-12

¹¹ And he saith unto them, Whosoever shall put away his wife, and marry another, committeth adultery against her.

¹² And if a woman shall put away her husband, and be married to another, she committeth adultery.

> Divorce was never in the perfect plan or will of God. Scripturally speaking, marriage is a life-long covenant. This is especially important to emphasize in a culture where marriages are so easily dissolved. The Word of God cites clear conditions for divorce.

1 Corinthians 7:10-17

¹⁰ And unto the married I command, yet not I, but the Lord, Let not the wife depart from her husband:

¹¹ But and if she depart, let her remain unmarried or be reconciled to her husband: and let not the husband put away his wife.

¹² But to the rest speak I, not the Lord: If any brother hath a wife that believeth not, and she be pleased to dwell with him, let him not put her away.

¹³ And the woman which hath an husband that believeth not, and if he be pleased to dwell with her, let her not leave him.

¹⁴ For the unbelieving husband is sanctified by the wife, and the unbelieving wife is sanctified by the husband: else were your children unclean; but now are they holy.

¹⁵ But if the unbelieving depart, let him depart. A brother or a sister is not under bondage in such cases: but God hath called us to peace.

¹⁶ For what knowest thou, O wife, whether thou shalt save thy husband? or how knowest thou, O man, whether thou shalt save thy wife?

¹⁷ But as God hath distributed to every man, as the Lord hath called every one, so let him walk. And so ordain I in all churches.

> The Word provides guidance on remaining in the marriage or being "put away" from the marriage. My experience tells me no one should be quick to walk away from a marriage because (to paraphrase verse 16 above) how do you know whether you can save the marriage unless you make every effort to reconcile and sustain the covenant relationship.

IN CLOSING

Thank you for considering the information presented in this book. As I said, it represents my insights and observations gained through years of pastoral counseling. It is my fervent prayer that this book provides life-giving direction and Godly counsel.

Please take courage and proceed with Pre-Marriage Counseling before embarking on the challenging journey of marriage. It will not be easy but your candid discussions will:

- Eliminate the worry that something you've kept to yourself will be discovered later;
- Give you an immeasurable peace that will certainly follow laying down that burden; and,
- Position your marriage for an incredible level of intimacy that comes from complete trust flowing from the reassurance that you truly know each other.

And know that even after having participated in extensive Pre-Marriage Counseling, you will still face challenges in your marriage that can be overcome by continuing to practice the candid communication skills you have developed together during this process.

APPENDIX I

Pre-Marriage Counseling Steps

1. Read and discuss Coming Together with Faith *(see Chapter 6)* to understand what the Bible says about marriage.

2. Complete the "Must Have Conversations" process.

    a. Each of you completes The Pre-Marriage Discussion Guide worksheet independently over a two-week period *(see Appendix II)*.

    b. After completion, share your answers with each other to identify areas of agreement and areas of conflict/ differences to talk through. You may find it helpful to use the table provided (see Appendix III) to capture the details regarding any concerns/differences that you need to work through.

    c. Attempt to reconcile areas of conflict/differences in conversation over a three-week period or as long as necessary. This work of speaking candidly and actively listening can be very emotional and challenging. Please remember the importance of choosing words carefully and being flexible.

    d. Consider your option to involve the pastor in mediating conflicts/differences that you have not been able to resolve. In some cases the result is a clear agreement to disagree so mediation is not requested. Be aware that issue is more than likely to come up over and over in the future.

3. Reach a decision to stop or proceed. It is not an easy thing to decide which way to go as you encounter the swirl of information and emotion in this process. Do we part ways here or do we go on? Can our relationship become what we both want? Can we work through the issues? As we do, will our love survive?

4. Inform the pastor of your thinking at this point and if the decision is to continue with your plan to marry, proceed with the following steps.

5. Develop a Marriage Mission Statement and draft your marriage vows (see *Appendix IV*).

   a. Each of you draft a summary of the aims and values of the marriage.
   b. Work together to merge the content into one statement, reconciling any differences.
   c. Review the traditional and sample personalized marriage vows. Draft your personalized vows, if desired.

6. Begin developing your first-year budget *(see Appendix V)*.

7. Pastor meets with husband candidate for practical discussion.

8. Pastor's wife, or female counselor, meets with wife candidate for practical discussion.

9. Meet in a final joint session with your pastor.

   a. Thoroughly review your marriage vows to ensure you both fully understand the commitment you are making.
   b. Confirm your decision to proceed with the marriage or go your separate ways.
   c. If the decision is to marry, discuss your personal wishes regarding the marriage ceremony including finalizing the marriage vows.

APPENDIX II

Pre-Marriage Discussion
Guide Worksheet

The Pre-Marriage Discussion Guide

The Marriage

1. Current marital status: (check all applicable categories)

    ___Never Been Married
    ___Married (process stops)
    ___Separated (process stops)
    ___Divorced (provide copy of divorce decree(s)
    ___Divorced (remarrying the same person)
    ___Widowed (provide copy of death certificate(s)

2. If divorced, what was the contributing issue(s)?

    How can you ensure it will not impact your impending marriage?

3. In your own words, what does marriage mean to you?

4. What specific actions or behaviors would fulfill marriage as you perceive it should be?

5. What are your expectations for the marriage?
   First year?

   Long term?

6. With regard to commitment to this marriage, what things would cause the marriage to dissolve emotionally or legally? Explain.

Money and Property

1. Where will we live after the marriage?

2. How will you handle your money?

   Individual bank accounts? Joint bank accounts?

3. How will household expenses be shared?

4. What kind of expenditures should be approved by both parties in advance?

5. Do you believe in saving? How will you ensure saving goals will be met?

6. How will you handle property attained prior to marriage, e.g. real estate, cash, cars, investments, etc.?

7. How will you handle requests for loans from your family members?

   From friends?

Work

1. Does your future spouse have a job?
   Will he/she continue to work after you are married?

   What is your expectation regarding his or her work, e.g. hours worked?

2. What has been your track record relative to holding a job?

3. Do you plan to work during the marriage and what is your expectation, e.g. hours worked?

Education

1. What is the highest level of education you have attained?

2. Do you plan to continue your pursuit of education?

3. How do you intend to pay for it?

4. Will you be a part-time or full-time student?

5. If full-time, will not working be acceptable to your spouse?

Spending

1. How would you quantify your expenditures directly related to the courtship?

_____Low
_____High

2. Please check the applicable categories for those expenditures.

    ____Meals in restaurants
    ____Entertainment, e.g. movies, concerts
    ____Travel
    ____Other (please list)

3. Are you expecting those expenditures to continue after the marriage ceremony?

    ____Yes, at an even higher level
    ____Yes, at the same level
    ____Yes, at a significantly reduced level
    ____No, please explain

4. Is shopping an important aspect of your life?

    ____Yes
    ____No

5. Percentage wise, how would you quantify your spending by category?

    ____Clothing
    ____Food
    ____Travel
    ____Gifts
    ____Charitable giving

6. In the marriage my expenditures in these categories will

    ____Continue at the same levels
    ____Reduce substantially (Please explain.)

Physical Relationship

1. Do you agree that it is a fact that your appearance and that of your spouse will change as you age?
   How will you deal with the physical changes?

   Will you still love him or her? Are you concerned that your spouse's feelings may change if your appearance changes? Do you feel strongly that your love can endure through all the inevitable changes?

2. In terms of personal hygiene what are your expectations for your spouse?

3. As clearly as possible, in words you are comfortable with, what are your expectations of the sexual aspects of marriage? *This is not the time to be shy or reticent.*

4. What sexual acts are you uncomfortable with performing?

5. With regard to your sexual relationship, how will you deal with differences in expectations and levels of comfort?

6. Do you watch pornography/graphic sex?

   ____Yes
   ____No

How will you feel if your spouse watches pornography?

7. Have you been subjected to sexual, physical and/or emotional abuse at any time?

    ____Yes
    ____No

If yes, please explain.

8. Have you received care to address this trauma?

    ____Yes
    ____No

If yes, please explain.

9. Do you define yourself as heterosexual? Bi-Sexual? Homosexual?

Are there any issues relative to sexual identity that you need to disclose?

Has there been a time when you experienced internal struggle over your sexual preference or gender identification?

Do you have any questions about your future spouse's sexual identity?

Communications

1. Are you satisfied with the level of communication/conversation between the two of you now?

      ___Yes
      ___No

2. With regard to communication/conversation, how would you describe it?

3. What do you talk about when you are together?

4. What topics important to you are not talked about?

5. Do you feel you do most of the listening?

      ___Yes
      ___No

6. Do you have shared interests, hobbies or activities? Please list.

7. How will you handle inevitable conflicts with each other?

With family members?

With others?

8. What is your plan for ensuring you keep open dialogue throughout the marriage?

The Family

1. List all your children including adults and grandchildren:

2. Do either of you have dependent children that will live with you and your spouse?

   Do you have a visitation plan that includes the dependent child's parent? Explain.

3. Do you plan to have children together?

   ___Yes
   ___No

   How many?

When?

4. Do you have any physical issues that would preclude having children?

        ____Yes
        ____No

If yes, what are they?

If you find you're unable to conceive as a couple, how will this affect your relationship?

Will you consider adoption?

5. What are your beliefs about disciplining children?

6. When needed, how will discipline be accomplished?

7. Will others be allowed to discipline your children, e.g., family members, friends, etc.?

8. If applicable, how do you feel about your husband/wife disciplining your children by another man/woman?

Has your agreement been communicated to the children?

Your Extended Family

1. Who are your parents?

   Are they still living?

2. How would you describe your relationship with your father?

3. How would you describe your relationship with your mother?

4. Do you have siblings? If so, describe your relationship with each sibling.

5. How would you describe your relationship with your grandparents?

6. Share a significant memory of each of your parents, grandparents and siblings:

7. How will you deal with your spouse's parents?

With his/her children and grandchildren?

With his/her siblings?

8. What is your expectation regarding where you will spend holidays?

9. How will the two of you establish your own family's customs?

Religion

1. What is your religious affiliation?
   What is your spiritual status?

2. How often do you attend church? How much time weekly do you spend in church/religious activities?

   Will this change after the marriage?

3. How do you feel about your spouse's time commitment to participating in church/religious activities?

4. Have you committed your life to Christ? Why or why not?

5. If your spouse does not share your religious beliefs or has not made a commitment to Christ, how will you deal with the inevitable conflict?

6. Have you studied Biblical teachings regarding marriage? *(See Chapter 6: Coming Together with Faith)*

Which of these Bible verses are important to you?

Are there verses that you are concerned about applying in your marriage? Explain.

7. Are there activities that you are expected to participate in with your future spouse that <u>conflict</u> with your spiritual beliefs?

Does he or she understand and accept your position?

Financial Disclosure

1. How much debt do you currently have? Delineate amounts and sources. Include any personal loans, mortgages, credit cards, unsecured loans, alimony, child support and any informal/formal agreements you have entered into to provide financial support.

2. Do you currently have any liens or unsettled judgments? Explain.

3. Attach a copy of your credit report (current within the last 30 days).

4. My credit rating is:

    ____Excellent
    ____Good
    ____Fair
    ____Poor

    Is there anything omitted from the credit report that should be disclosed?

5. Have you ever filed for bankruptcy?
   When?

Status?

6. Are you current on state and federal income tax returns and payments?

   If not, explain.

7. Are you under tax audit or a payment plan with either state or federal?

8. Disclose any bad financial behaviors that you have practiced in the past <u>and</u> your current thinking and practices pertaining to those past practices.

9. Do you have life insurance?

   Who are the beneficiaries?

   Will this change after marriage?

10. How will assets accumulated before the marriage be distributed upon your death?

11. Do you have a will?

12. How will assets accumulated during our marriage be distributed?

Political Affiliation

1. How do you classify yourself?

    ___Democrat
    ___Republican
    ___Independent
    ___Other, please specify_____

2. Do you have any strongly held political opinions?

3. If your opinions differ from those of your future spouse, how will you manage the inevitable conflicts?

Housework and Property Maintenance

1. What is your expectation regarding who will take care of day-to-day routine housework and maintenance (cooking, cleaning, washing dishes, mowing, etc.)?

2. How much time do you anticipate you will spend on these tasks each week?

Medical/Health

1. Do you have any on-going medical (physical and/or mental health) conditions?

2. Do you need to take prescribed medications?

3. Do you have any conditions that may preclude you from having children or performing sexually?

4. Are you now, or have you been, in recovery for an addiction? If so, explain any support that would be helpful to you.

Criminal History

1. Have you ever been arrested?

    ___Yes
    ___No

    If yes, why? When?

2. Have you served time in prison?

    ___Yes
    ___No

    If yes, why? When?

3. Do you currently have any outstanding issues of a criminal nature? Explain.

4. Attach a copy of your police report current within the last 30 days.

Reflections

1. If you could change anything about your past what would it be?

2. Do you have aspirations that you still hope to achieve?

3. Is there anything you can think of that might become a source of dispute in the future? Please disclose.

4. In what way do you hope to enhance your future spouse's life?

    How has he/she enhanced your life so far?

APPENDIX III

Table for Capturing Issues to be Resolved

Capturing Issues to be Resolved	
Consider carefully: Is there true agreement versus a decision to ignore the difference of opinion so as not to disturb plans? Think through what it will mean to live with the difference of opinion for a lifetime. The decision to proceed or not proceed should not be made on the basis of plans already made or what others will think. Only *you* have to live with the daily consequences of your decision.	
The Marriage	
Concerns/Differences:	Outcome: ☐ Agreement reached Explain briefly: ☐ Decision to live with difference of opinion ☐ Decision not to proceed

Money and Property	
Concerns/Differences:	Outcome: ☐ Agreement reached Explain briefly: ☐ Decision to live with difference of opinion ☐ Decision not to proceed

Work	
Concerns/Differences:	Outcome: ☐ Agreement reached Explain briefly: ☐ Decision to live with difference of opinion ☐ Decision not to proceed

Education	
Concerns/Differences:	Outcome: ☐ Agreement reached Explain briefly: ☐ Decision to live with difference of opinion ☐ Decision not to proceed

Spending	
Concerns/Differences:	Outcome: ☐ Agreement reached Explain briefly: ☐ Decision to live with difference of opinion ☐ Decision not to proceed

Physical Relationship	
Concerns/Differences:	Outcome: ☐ Agreement reached Explain briefly: ☐ Decision to live with difference of opinion ☐ Decision not to proceed

Communications	
Concerns/Differences:	Outcome: ☐ Agreement reached Explain briefly: ☐ Decision to live with difference of opinion ☐ Decision not to proceed

The Family	
Concerns/Differences:	Outcome: ☐ Agreement reached Explain briefly: ☐ Decision to live with difference of opinion ☐ Decision not to proceed

Your Extended Family	
Concerns/Differences:	Outcome: ☐ Agreement reached Explain briefly: ☐ Decision to live with difference of opinion ☐ Decision not to proceed

Religion	
Concerns/Differences:	Outcome: ☐ Agreement reached Explain briefly: ☐ Decision to live with difference of opinion ☐ Decision not to proceed

Financial Disclosure	
Concerns/Differences:	Outcome: ☐ Agreement reached Explain briefly: ☐ Decision to live with difference of opinion ☐ Decision not to proceed

Political Affiliation	
Concerns/Differences:	Outcome: ☐ Agreement reached Explain briefly: ☐ Decision to live with difference of opinion ☐ Decision not to proceed

Housework and Property Maintenance	
Concerns/Differences:	Outcome: ☐ Agreement reached Explain briefly: ☐ Decision to live with difference of opinion ☐ Decision not to proceed

Medical/Health	
Concerns/Differences:	Outcome: ☐ Agreement reached Explain briefly: ☐ Decision to live with difference of opinion ☐ Decision not to proceed
Criminal History	
Concerns/Differences:	Outcome: ☐ Agreement reached Explain briefly: ☐ Decision to live with difference of opinion ☐ Decision not to proceed
Reflections	
Concerns/Differences:	Outcome: ☐ Agreement reached Explain briefly: ☐ Decision to live with difference of opinion ☐ Decision not to proceed
Decision	
Concluding thoughts:	☐ Proceed with marriage ☐ Seek mediation ☐ Postpone wedding ☐ Cancel wedding

It is not an easy thing to decide which way to go as you encounter the swirl of information and emotion in this process. Do we part ways here or do we go on? Can our relationship become what we both want? Can we work through the issues? As we do, will our love survive? Regardless of the decision you make, remember that you have accomplished an important step in your journey: to truly know each other.

APPENDIX IV

Our Mission Statement
and Marriage Vows

Mission Statement

Complete the following, working individually:

1. What are our aims in getting married? What can we achieve together in life that we cannot achieve alone?

2. What are our basic values?

3. Considering the Bible verses discussed in Chapter 6 *(see your notes in Appendix II under Religion)*, which one(s) would you choose to serve as guideposts for the marriage?

4. Draft a Mission Statement

Our mission is to establish a home where God is honored, where love is the guiding principle, where there is mutual respect and open communication, where commitments are met in a timely way, and where individual and family fulfillment are valued and enabled.

Marriage Vows

You may choose traditional vows or personalize the vows. If you personalize them, you may repeat the same vows or express unique vows.

1. Review the sample marriage vows below.
2. Draft your marriage vows, working individually.

Sample Traditional Marriage Vows

Wilt thou have this Woman to thy wedded wife, to live together after God's ordinance in the holy estate of matrimony? Wilt thou love her, comfort her, honor, and keep her, in sickness and in health; and, forsaking all others, keep thee only unto her, so long as ye both shall live?

The man shall answer, I will.

Wilt thou have this Man to thy wedded husband, to live together after God's ordinance in the holy estate of matrimony? Wilt thou obey him and serve him, love, honor and keep him, in sickness and in health; and, forsaking all others, keep thee only unto him, so long as ye both shall live?

The woman shall answer, I will.

Final Mission Statement and Marriage Vows

Working together, finalize your Mission Statement and Marriage Vows.

Our Marriage

The Mission Statement for Our Marriage:

Our Basic Core Values are:

We will follow God's Word faithfully:

We pledge to honor our vows:

Bride's vows:

Groom's vows:

APPENDIX V

Budget for Our First Year

Understanding Household Income and Expenses

Before the Wedding			
This table may assist you in discussing spending and other budget items in Appendix I.			
INCOME	His	Hers	Total
Salary	$	$	$
Tips	$	$	$
	$	$	$
	$	$	$
Total	$	$	$
EXPENSES	His	Hers	Total
Rent/Mortgage			
Clothing	$	$	$
Food			
Travel	$	$	$
Gifts	$	$	$
Charitable giving	$	$	$
Amount to Savings	$	$	$
	$	$	$
	$	$	$
	$	$	$

Total	$	$	$
Combined Totals			
Income	$	$	$
Expenses	$	$	$
Income - Expenses	$	$	$

Disclosing Financial Responsibilities

Source	His	Hers	Total
Visa Balance	$	$	$
Discover Balance	$	$	$
Other Credit Card	$	$	$
Personal Loan	$	$	$
Unsecured Loan	$	$	$
Mortgage	$	$	$
Alimony	$	$	$
Child Support	$	$	$
Medical Bills	$	$	$
Student Loans	$	$	$
Other	$	$	$
	$	$	$
	$	$	$

Identifying Other Sources of Income

Source	His	Hers	Total
Savings Account	$	$	$
Life Insurance	$	$	$
401(k) Plan	$	$	$
Stocks/Bonds	$	$	$
Other	$	$	$

	$	$	$
	$	$	$
	$	$	$

Estimating a Monthly Budget

After the Wedding

Following your discussion about finances, you may use this table to draft a household budget based on your habits before the wedding and your pre-marriage agreements.

INCOME	His	Hers	Total
Salary/Tips	$	$	$
Interest	$	$	$
Other	$	$	$
Total	$	$	$
EXPENSES	His	Hers	Total
Rent/Mortgage	$	$	$
Utilities	$	$	$
Food	$	$	$
Clothing	$	$	$
Web/Cell	$	$	$
Gas, Travel	$	$	$
Childcare	$	$	$
Gifts	$	$	$
Charitable giving	$	$	$
Credit Card Payments	$	$	$
Amount to Savings	$	$	$
Personal	$	$	$
Other	$	$	$
Total	$	$	$
TOGETHER			
Total Income	$	$	$

Total Expenses	$	$	$
Income - Expenses	$	$	$

Learning from Experience

Tracking Actual Income and Expenses

Consider taking a small spiral notepad with you so you can track where the money goes. If changes in spending or other choices need to be made, consider each other's feelings, including responses in the pre-marriage discussion, to reach an agreement.

INCOME	Month 1	Month 2	Month 3
Salary/Tips	$	$	$
Interest	$	$	$
Other	$	$	$
Total	$	$	$
EXPENSES	Month 1	Month 2	Month 3
Rent/Mortgage	$	$	$
Utilities	$	$	$
Food	$	$	$
Clothing	$	$	$
Web/Cell	$	$	$
Gas, Travel	$	$	$
Childcare	$	$	$
Gifts	$	$	$
Charitable giving	$	$	$
Credit Card Payments	$	$	$
Amount to Savings	$	$	$
Personal	$	$	$
Other	$	$	$
Total	$	$	$

BALANCE			
Total Income	$	$	$
Total Expenses	$	$	$
Income - Expenses	$	$	$

Finalizing the Budget

After the Wedding

Based on your discussions, develop a final budget to follow for the rest of the first year, using this form or other tools, e.g., https://docs.google.com/spreadsheets or https://mint.intuit.com/.

INCOME	Budgeted	Actual Month 4	Actual Month 5
Salary/Tips	$	$	$
Interest	$	$	$
Other	$	$	$
Total	$	$	$
EXPENSES	His	Hers	Total
Rent/Mortgage	$	$	$
Utilities	$	$	$
Food	$	$	$
Clothing	$	$	$
Web/Cell	$	$	$
Gas, Travel	$	$	$
Childcare	$	$	$
Gifts	$	$	$
Charitable giving	$	$	$
Credit Card Payments	$	$	$
Amount to Savings	$	$	$
Personal	$	$	$
Other	$	$	$
Total	$	$	$

BALANCE			
Total Income	$	$	$
Total Expenses	$	$	$
Income - Expenses	$	$	$

ACKNOWLEDGMENTS

I must formally express my appreciation for those individuals who graciously committed time and effort in reviewing and editing this book:

- Valerie Atkins, B.A., M.A., M.Ed., LPC
- Pastor Wayne M. Bass, B.A., M.A., M.R.E.
- Bishop Eric L. Butler, B.S., M.S., Senior Pastor
- Timothy P. Foster, B.A.
- Paula C. Hearn, B.A., M.A., MBA, SPHR, CPC
- Doris P. Wade, B.A., M.Ed.

ABOUT THE AUTHOR

 Edwin C. Bass has served as the Senior Pastor of The Empowered Church, Church of God in Christ for thirty years. He has also served at times as Senior Vice President, Sales & Marketing, for Alliance Blue Cross Blue Shield as well as Chief Operating Officer of the Church of God in Christ, Inc.

In each role, he has witnessed the devastating effect on marriages when partners fail to communicate fully prior to entering the marriage covenant. On the other hand, he has observed that when partners start out the marriage with open communication, they have set the standard for how they will communicate throughout the marriage. He is committed to providing pre-marriage counseling that facilitates intentional, in-depth communication between individuals contemplating marriage.

Printed in the United States
by Baker & Taylor Publisher Services